OUR LIFE BEFORE MARS

Renee de la Roche-Zhu

Liminal Press

Copyright © 2025 Renee de la Roche-Zhu

All rights reserved

The characters and events portrayed in this book are fictitious. Any similarity to real persons, living or dead, is coincidental and not intended by the author.

A number of poems in this collection were originally published by Liminal Press in French Restaurant (March 2024). These appear here either in their original form or in revised editions, alongside new, previously unpublished work.

No part of this book may be reproduced, or stored in a retrieval system, or transmitted in any form or by any means, electronic, mechanical, photocopying, recording, or otherwise, without express written permission of the publisher.

ISBN-13: 979-8-218-66752-8

Cover design by: M. R. Cavendish

Printed in the United States of America

To my friends and family. To fiction that is truer than life, and life that is falser than fiction

What is the meaning of life? That was all – a simple question; one that tended to close in on one with years, the great revelation had never come. The great revelation perhaps never did come. Instead, there were little daily miracles, illuminations, matches struck unexpectedly in the dark; here was one.

VIRGINIA WOOLF, TO THE LIGHTHOUSE

CONTENTS

Title Page
Copyright
Dedication
Epigraph
Introduction
I. Boston   2
The Miasma of Us   3
Thirties   6
Atonement   9
Our Metamodernity   12
Our Life Before Mars   14
Act of Survival   17
I Migrate towards the Fog   19
Birthday Wish   21
II. Los Angeles   24
Exit Interview from the Extinction Scene   25
That Sunday, That Summer   28

Quail Eggs	31
Presently (soon)	33
Trip to Japan	34
The Gazelle	36
Los Angeles, The City in Which I Loved You	39
III. New York / After the Pandemic	43
Of Witch-hazel, Thickening	44
Three Lives	46
French Restaurant	49
Days on Mars	52
It Was Later than I Thought	54
Girl from the Pale Blue Dot	56
Prince Gallery Hotel, À La Anne Sexton	58
A Woman Is a Woman	60
J.W.M. Turner	62
It's Lonely to Be on Earth Now	64
IV. New York / During the Pandemic	66
My Future	67
Youth	69
So Long, Ms. First Aid	71
Betelgeuse, See You at Sunset	73
Vague d'Azur	74
風の歌を聴け	75
Georgia O'Keeffe, Ms. Allergic to Cheese	78

Sweet as Summer, Then Sweeter	81
Dream a Dream, Here's a Scene	82
V. London	84
You'll Eat a Hamburger, In Fact	85
The Arrow	87
Ted Hughes	89
Army of Me	91
Dancing with Father John Misty #2	94
One Day	96
VI. Tokyo	98
The Greatest	99
After the After	101
Villefranche-sur-Mer	102
Le Grand Brouillard	103
Ground Control to Major Golightly	104
Scream	105
Tokyo Belle de Jour	106
Tokyo, Mon Amour	107
VIi. Hong Kong	109
Souvenir	110
Hunter S. Thompson	111
The Life Before Us	112
Afterword	116
About The Author	118

Books By This Author

INTRODUCTION

This collection, a continuation of the spirit first captured in *French Restaurant* (Liminal Press, March 2024), is a meditation on how we carry meaning across geographies, relationships, and selves – how we fragment, reassemble, and evolve while living in motion.

Structured in loose reverse chronology (and designed to be readable both forwards and backwards), these chapters of poems trace a woman's migrations across six cities through six years, charting themes of *grief and inheritance, ambition and self-authorship, intimacy and independence* – and at their core, *the search for meaning*. Written in New York, London, Tokyo, Hong Kong, Los Angeles, Boston, and other liminal spaces, *Our Life Before Mars* is both a record of time and a refusal to obey its linearity:

In **Hong Kong**, the work wrestles with *lineage and fracture*, both personal and political, as the speaker first arrives during the height of the city's unprecedented civil unrest, set against the backdrop of its complicated history (e.g., *Souvenir*). When she returns five years later, the verses reflect a shifting sense of identity, tracing how personal and cultural legacies are inherited and carried forward (e.g., *The Life Before Us*).

In **Tokyo**, *displacement and desire* are deeply intertwined. The speaker first encounters the city through intimacy – cinematic and electric (e.g., *Tokyo Belle de Jour*). The poems capture both the ache to be seen and the temptation to disappear (e.g., *The Greatest*) as an avoidant. In a more fundamental way, perhaps made clearer in returns to the city versus the initial year of exploration (e.g., *Tokyo Mon Amour*), Tokyo becomes a city of private reinvention and curated solitude away from the "mainstream" – an alternative answer to the question: *what kind of life should we live and is worth living?*

In **London**, which the speaker visits as an adult, the verses navigate *memory and fracture* – the way a global upbringing leaves a person scattered across multiple versions of home both in past and present tense (e.g., *Army of Me*). London as a city becomes a foil – creating the room for a retrospective gaze, one attuned to contradiction and quietly resistant to nostalgia's distortions (e.g., *The Arrow*). It is also where the speaker, with a heart in transition, begins to accept the weight of love, not just its benefits (e.g., *You'll Eat a Hamburger, In Fact*).

In **New York**, the tone shifts toward *survival and striving*. These poems inhabit a second coming – a return during the pandemic to the speaker's "second home," prompted by familial obligation (e.g., *So Long, Ms. First Aid*) – and ultimately reckon with the weight of ambition (e.g., *A Woman Is a Woman*). However, the city, once a fountain of vitality and promise, no longer offers the same renewal. Yet the *self-making* still takes place – still restless (e.g., *Hear the Wind Sing*), and still performative (e.g., *My Future*). There is also a pivot towards wry detachment as a coping mechanism – a burgeoning flirtation with nihilistic self-awareness (e.g., *Georgia O'Keefe, Ms. Allergic to Cheese*) as she grapples with loss.

The poems after the pandemic pinpoint both professional ascent and emotional undoing. Beneath them is a quiet grief: the decision to leave Tokyo – a life not fully explored – was not made entirely for herself, and hence its cost lingers – perhaps even more clearly with the passage of time (e.g., *It Was Later Than I Thought*). There is another, more vital kind of grief, too – that of familial loss (e.g., *It's Lonely to Be on Earth Now*) – which begins to overshadow even the brightness of friendship and love. And yet those relationships, despite being tested, reveal their strength: what remains is not fantasy or escape, but resilience – of being present in the aftermath (e.g., *Days on Mars*).

In **Los Angeles**, the poems navigate *transition and reorientation* – confronting the constitution of past careers (e.g., *Exit Interview from the Extinction Scene*), negotiating the terms of personal and cultural identity (e.g., *That Sunday, That Summer*), and exploring the depth of emotional growth (e.g., *Quail Eggs*). The terrain is sun-drenched but uncertain. The speaker arrives in search of a gentler path forward – one that allows her to come home (e.g., *Trip to Japan*). Most importantly, these verses loosen the grip of old narratives and entertain the possibility that change may be quiet, slow, and elemental (e.g., *Presently (soon)*). And for the first time, perhaps, *love* endures – one that not only survives migration but also takes root in the desert (e.g., *Los Angles, The City in Which I Loved You*).

Then, in **Boston**, the poems soften. A chapter that unfolds with *clarity and stillness* – one that embraces aging with calm (e.g., *Thirties*), chooses presence over departure (e.g., *Act of Survival, Our Life Before Mars*), and finds liberation not in the meaningless striving for prestige but in rootedness (e.g., *The Miasma of Us*). These poems are less stylized, more interior, and newly attuned to the importance of the quotidian. They also take attendance of the shifting architectures of society – where late-stage ambition, inherited histories, and quiet civilizational fatigue form the backdrop to how we evolve as our metamodern selves (e.g., *Our Metamodernity, Atonement*), oscillating between striving and surrender. In their totality, they mark an arrival – not to a place, but to a new relationship with the self: a self no longer seducing the mirror but inhabiting it.

From Tokyo to Boston, thus, the poetic voice undoubtedly evolves – from one shaped by the thrills and agonies of ambition, romance, and displacement to one that hinges on philosophical clarity, self-authorship, and stillness.

The questions deepen, too: *What do we inherit? What do we try to outrun? How do we grow older – without turning away? What do we choose to stay for, when we could always depart?*

These poems are meant as a map of emotional and philosophical terrain – a record of the *ordinary* and the *epic* unfolding quietly side by side. Boston is not the endpoint, either, but the stop before "Mars" – i.e., the next migration, the next self. These poems, in that sense, are a document of becoming. Of life – before the next big transformation.

Boston, April 2025

RENEE DE LA ROCHE-ZHU

Our Life Before Mars

I. BOSTON

THE MIASMA OF US

Where's the lighthouse where You are?
What about the weather?
I used to think, when the reward for the
Pie-eating contest is more pie,
Eight times a week on the pavement, are You
A bookmark in my field of meandering prose, or,
When the plane
Crashes inevitably,
The work of Achievement, or History
Itself?

The fog – it does not lift
Easily in Boston. The Back Bay
Mews scintillate with houses of distinct glories
For the day kneels forward, quietly, as the river
Does. And in its steady ongoings, I lose sight of the lanterns on
A dark lane in New York or Tokyo – the aspiration towards
Greatness in a different tonality – hunting from dawn to dusk, my mind
With a rapidity to it. I seek – as I grow older – to cease the
Re-litigation of
The past

In vain, for streets, then
Bridges of You crowd towards me

OUR LIFE BEFORE MARS

Pushing architecture of ancient and new into a
Standstill. I arrest traffic, or time
Itself, to pause for a look
Of You. Of fissured atoms that fill my chawanmushi
Bowls as they do emails sent in Polaris Lounges –
That constitute this
Miasma of us – that which bears
No name

You mailed me a package from Your skyscraper
House in my bizzarro dream – Financial District
Or Roppongi – I am no longer sure of it
It had a fan booklet You sent to
Jackie Chan when You were four and absurd
Childhood assertions that You'd take over the Retirement industry
In it You also apologized to me seminally
For not knowing what it is You really wanted, except
That first time in 2022, when I wasn't ready. When I told You grief
Was coming into me, like wind

But even grief itself wasn't really the problem
It was You – a vessel of supposed wisdom for the ambitious. Our days
Colored by the distinct atrocity of Your ambivalence
Yet this is no longer an indictment, my love
I am tired of listening to Your Five-Year Plans, keeping what I can of You
Happy now that You'll never know
That my father named me Artemis – so I can be both substance,
And vessel for the wilderness. And the danger
Of the road not travelled is that it haunts you, until you learn

RENEE DE LA ROCHE-ZHU

How to traverse it, like wind

Boston, February 2025

THIRTIES

I put on Shintaro Sakamoto after dinner, which we
Both enjoy, mercurial yet boundless
Unlike Mahler – overly elegiac for a rainy
Spring night where the fog stretches out
Like a black cat by the window. Ambulances blare
Their way down the avenue with the "patience" of newborns
Look, the bread is sliced on the cutting board, as the
Decade unwinds into years, which fissure
Into quarters, and then into months
And days. The peaches are preserved
In jars. A child bends down to pick up a yellow mango. Now that
We are in our thirties – the mail
Piles up

Except I've never loved more than now the shape
Of my body. How I've drained my legs of energy, then
Mechanized them
With a cocktail of ferality and wilderness
I'm not saying my steps are finally light, but my
Waist is now sculpted with the precision
Of a hunter's dream. And my
Countenance, more varied and awake than my twenties –
Like the horizon that can grow overcast or clear, except I'm no longer
Disconcerted by lightning that

Makes me see. I stand in front of a mirror, combing hinoki conditioner
Through the ends of my hair, waiting for the
Advent of wrinkles

For they are not on my face. Not yet. I look for their
Arrival not out of fear – but to measure how far I've travelled
From home. From myself. I keep looking, my fingers
Tracing against my neck – where a few lines
Run like vacant streets
At night. Directions perplex me, so I keep pacing
Until I reach the crest of my clavicle bones. Until I am near
The opening and closing of my heart. I knock on it – like
Onlookers near a church. For I know, this, too
Is the war
The looking. Tracing. Knocking. I keep marching, towards
The upside down pyramid – for I've learned how to die, and
Get free

I think, now,
I'm finally on the right side of the war. I tell myself to be
Still – that if all that's left to do
Is live
And die. Then what is the rush? For there is
Something beautiful about stillness
About staying. In a body. In a room. In the
Long, unwinding wait for the hours, for children –
Or the decision not to have them. I don't have a Five-Year
Plan, or a manifesto – but I have a prosciutto sandwich in my right
Hand. So let me enter the lion's den, and discover

Molasses. Let me grow older
There

Boston, April 2025

ATONEMENT

In the middle of the morning, not
Night, a rogue river runs upstream towards the prancing
Flamingoes on the hills of Eastbourne
Where a holiday house of little scale stands
With malevolent softness
In the grand scheme of things, away from the domes that lie
Dormant in London, guarded under mist. Except this isn't the
Imaginary house in the film I watched at thirteen
Starring Keira Knightley. This is one of childhood, of
Its generational architecture, and its fissures

Along Seven Sisters beach
Black sands scintillate with the veiled
Truths of yesteryear. Here father taught me
Love carries interests. A 'first principle' of monumental
Degree. A lie unbeknownst to five-year-old me
Riding lessons or a baby grand piano, he always asked,
"What will you give me, in return?" For fatherhood is hardly a
Home in every town, but the edge of a desert called
Ambition, against which I chafe. I chafe
No charming smile. No malachite eyes

I think about the morning before my first
Day of school. How he rushed me through breakfast

OUR LIFE BEFORE MARS

While he scanned the *Financial Times*. The fog wouldn't
Lift that morning – yet a sadness – an obesity of it –
Filled the air. Thickening, like paint
I think about the machines that beeped quietly
Next to him before he was gone. The truth, if the
Word deserves a passport, is I never had anything to
Give him except another version of history. One that
He wanted to hear

Father used to teach me the art of
Disentanglement. Of hunting prey of their
Own choosing. I think about how we used to sit at
China Tang at the Dorchester – him asking me
What I want to eat. I am eleven. We love the Dungeness
Crab so much – I think about how he peels them for me, teaching
Me how to get the meat out. *Fully.* I think about how I
Held my heart close to him as we brushed our teeth
In front of the mirror. Rinse and repeat, until one of us
Is met with death – the other shoe that drops, too quickly

I would love to walk to the cliffs with you, father,
Or the post office. I miss you in your long winter coat, and
The father-daughter Mahler No.5 *Adagietto* 'sing-along' when I
Was a little girl. But you edged into oblivion like
A shooting star, bursting into a cascade of sparks
Standing at your eulogy, with terrors in my stomach I'm
Unable to name, I thought about those who buy groceries
On Friday nights. Those making tea in the quiet morning
Light of their kitchen. Those who you'd laugh at, who guard

RENEE DE LA ROCHE-ZHU

Their lives with a vortex at the core. Those not unlike me

Near the shore the waves come and go with ease – this
Is no longer a stormy rendering of the past, but one
With measured objectivity. "I will love you, *again*," I answer
You twenty-something years later. For
How do we author our creator's death? How do we
Promise to be happy? So, today I rise, I walk
I read, I breathe
I say to the sea – father, wherein lies
Your song? For I am lost at home in the world
In your name

Boston, January 2025

OUR METAMODERNITY

I buy flowers from the store on the corner from
This Japanese woman in a polka dot
Dress who pretends she does not
Recognize me, nor the versions of tales on my face –
On some days I show up with cloudy eyeshadow, on others
With light rouge of pure elation. But she just
Wraps the flowers in tissue paper. White
Hydrangeas mostly, and sometimes orange tulips
She does not bore us with small talk. But I don't think
It's because her English isn't very good. I think in a way
She is omniscient and inscrutable at once – the kind of woman
Who can be a billion botanical gardens to the restless. We dance
This silent dance. We keep up this charade. I pay her a bit extra
Each time, for she affords me the grace that
Even my family couldn't give me on good days, or you
On slightly worse ones

For I need not discuss with her how a snowstorm
Wailed over Charles River, or once
Over the Thames. The Hudson. Not the
Wildfires that almost burned down my house
In Pasadena, or the imaginary Nankai Earthquake that
Shook our core on the slowed-down Shinkansen on August 17,
2024. Not the war on the other side of the world, or the ones

RENEE DE LA ROCHE-ZHU

Within, marinating up the genetic tree to the Cultural Revolution, or
Qin Dynasty. For in me, the passage of time beats with the
Alacrity of a proximal bomb – if I cannot learn to give
More than I was taught as a child. If I cannot forgive
My father and remain a fugitive to my own
Beating heart. If I cannot be certain of Life's worth. It's barely
Been a quarter since 2024, but I'm tired. Everyone is
Tired. Every woman is tired of *becoming*

Today I dropped by the florist after work, with the usual
Exhaustion from the plotting and planning required in
A modern woman's voyage. I asked her for a dozen of
Birds of paradise. She looked surprised but remained silent –
The corner of her mouth moving with signs of recollecting. For she,
Too, is a body of memories, of endeavoring. She disappeared
Into the back and reemerged with a nice bunch – and in handing them
To me, she spoke for the first time – *What is it…you really want
To be?* Certain she could just be speaking about the flowers
Or the occasion that behooves them. I looked out the window at
The garden. Colorless. Spindled by the creeping
Limbs of winter. Of so-called change. I looked at the flood
In this world, standing in the way of the good life. And I
Thought about how I want to rule over
My flood. My chaos. I took the flowers from her hand, and told her,
I want to be the King

Boston, March 2025

OUR LIFE BEFORE MARS

We fought last night over something nonsensical – or perhaps
Deeply existential, according to the knot
In my amygdala. And if the argument
Were a girl, she wasn't known for her beauty, Or mercy
Outside the window on Traveler Street people
Have put on garments of indifference
In fear of the advent of happiness
To get through winter, in love with the hieroglyphs
Of pain

Breakfast for two
Coffee for one
You still pour my tea and stir the almond milk in with ease
For a moment I thought I've seen men like you on the silver
Screen – consistent yet stubborn
Are our rituals governed by artifice
And "should be"s
Or are they breathing artifacts of us
Those of the bedrock of our cosmic
Entanglement

I'm still ensnared by my own curse
But you go buy a nice wine over in *Kairos*
Time, and suggest we watch a "thriller"

RENEE DE LA ROCHE-ZHU

That doesn't disappoint
No one steals the show – silence meanders like time does
Yet you still give me
Everything
I listen to the sound of you washing
Vegetables in the kitchen
It sounds like singing

And I think – when will I finally be through with me?
Until the next cloud I mount
Above us, or until I battle you to death
As I do
My father
I can't help it – like how
The years go by, and lightning grows jagged into the
Sky like antlers. And how young men across the world
Go to war
Without remedy

The kettle whistles – you ask me to choose a tea
It hit me suddenly
Perhaps we made it work
In a past life
And now, is not now
But the future
The one where we will have grown up to be our ancestors
In ancient cave paintings
And our life – is not Life, but a metamodern
Mythology

OUR LIFE BEFORE MARS

Cape Cod, December 2024

ACT OF SURVIVAL

And you put my shoes on for me at the door
Like you always do when I leave
The house, devoted as Humbert Humbert. Except
In this story – we are of the same age. Our days marked
By the limitless expanse of the crepuscular sky
But the aches in my bones still overwhelm me like sleet
In a quickening blizzard – those out of hypervigilance,
Marinating all the way to the root of childhood
"Once we get engaged," you say calmingly as
You tie my shoelaces, "we should just
Get married right away. Let's
Not wait"

I smile less like the woman on
The cover of a bridal magazine and more like
One at an airport terminal. I'm aware
Of the architecture of my heart – how
The left ventricle is made of salt and warmth
Like the sea, and how the right is cursed with a blue shadow – even in
Death, my father's grip only tightens. The hunter
Who taught me to negotiate first, love
Second. "One step at a time", I say like the woman who knocks on the door
Of her own church, who doesn't believe in the promise of

OUR LIFE BEFORE MARS

The heron. Who spots the deer
Miles ahead, unlike Jesus

Except what I really want to say is
I am afraid. That the big-eared boy on the
2nd floor will not make friends that last
A lifetime. That the French florist on the corner will no longer carry
Birds of paradise. That the wildfires of California
Will rage again this fall
That tomorrow you'd die on the way
To the grocery store
That I'd run out of words when I sit down
Five years from now at my orange typewriter. You'd call this
An act of survival – but as I close the door – I think maybe it is
An act of love

Brookline, April 2025

I MIGRATE TOWARDS THE FOG

You cut through a sea of mediocrity with
Grass blades that point towards you, but you don't
Speak of it to me, unlike of the furniture, out on
The terrace that darkens under the moon in its
Quiet chronology, which you placed, tasteful and
Homemade. I think about their stories of origin,
Of evolution. And how we will make it through
This world as we age

Young but with gravity in my pockets, you are
Quick to support me in this voyage in which
I wear florals without accident. Spring draws
Near, but lately the world dims as I step into it. How
Across the riverbank women my age no longer play with
Yellow flowers. Yet on my dress they decorate my mood, mercurial
Yet patient. I go to the Word of Mouth café for news
Updates nowadays – picking up quail eggs on the way

The end of winter ordains a new beginning
With green balconies. Beneath which lies the sea, where I
Once lived with white doves. But I am a little seashell
Now; my breeze comes from within – smooth like

OUR LIFE BEFORE MARS

Time, its dailiness, and its irrevocability
I migrate towards the fog as it nears the shore, unambiguous
Without tickets, the moon must rise, as I must one day
Board a boisterous train towards Mercury

Boston, March 2025

BIRTHDAY WISH

Happy Birthday. I said I would not burden myself,
Or you with clichés

Fill the spaces in between my words, and then
The hours with the prosperity

Of the minutiae. For the moon and the sun battled
For a long while, but we are now

More than before, masters of our secret
Language, its syntax held together by threads

Invisible to the calm of a breezed dawn
Children running on the pavement

Flourishing, now, at the inception of a
Martian age. For to be young, together,

Is to be at once intrepid
And tender. No, I'm not afraid

Of foreign boulevards, the inevitable Nankai
Earthquake

OUR LIFE BEFORE MARS

Of wind, thunder
Or rain

Except I am afraid of the maze, the one
In which I am entrapped in circular narratives

Where I am neither heroine nor villain – just a woman
With a black bird on her shoulder, who can no longer

Make her sorrow count. I wait in vain for you to extinguish
My flame when the Martian storm rages, but you are unable

To work as a firefighter, crippled by the parched riverbed
Of your own defense mechanisms. And I

Will have to carry my own bones and bury them
When I run out of seeds to replenish our

Garden. My sorrow is a big deal – and I am
A big deal. But I will put that aside now, and

Wish you a happy birthday. It's been five years
Since Phoebe Bridgers sang Kyoto, and four

Since Chemtrails over the Country Club. I know
Now the beauty of meeting for coffee with a friend

In the neighborhood, and the power of doing laundry
On Sundays, but I know not the telos of time

RENEE DE LA ROCHE-ZHU

But I hope it is not this. The spiraling duels between
Versions of childhood traumas – like those of our

DNA. For you don't yet know, despite the long road
I've had to travel, that one is not born, but rather

Inhabits a woman. It's 2025 now, and it's quiet
Out on Harvard Street. The population is tired of verbs

Like 'to-be.' So illuminate me, will the moon still
Rise? Will the stars have her blood on their hands

And wear the unrest as a flag? Is it too early for her
To leave, or too late for her to stay?

First written New York, May 2021
Revised Boston, April 2025

II. LOS ANGELES

EXIT INTERVIEW FROM THE EXTINCTION SCENE

Artemis, guide me now, in this time of unrest –
For I walk on unfamiliar roads charred by
Crimson twilight, advancing towards
Or is it away from the Sun?
I have not picked up the pen for ages, beset by
Sentence structures of mediocrity
Architected to fissure those with imagination
Into syllables
In my dream you wrote to me out of the blue
As the moon waned. I hadn't forgotten about you –
How you texted, when it rained in London, that
'You loved me like family.' The journalist that challenges
The superstructure of nonsense throughout my twenties

The Arizona mountainscape
Overwhelms me with notions
Of disparate lived realities – I am here, aren't I?
From Sedona to the Grand Canyon
The scenic train traverses through greatness of
A particular kind

OUR LIFE BEFORE MARS

I am unable to name it. I search for a vision
Of God in our rearview mirror, how she laughs
At eons of pain
My vision blears as I have a shuddering thought
About interest rates – I imagine you pulling up the FT
As I lunch at the local café in town, apologetic about
Asking for almond milk towards the waitress

At the edge of the Canyon, or is it under the
Sweeping, starry night sky
Ursa Major comes down to the plains to
Tell me a bedtime story. About when the
Town is silent, how he wants to die
And how death starts like
A dream, full of objects and the drumming on
Of desert winds. I ask if he's hungry for
A slice of shepherd's pie made with cactus. His eyes
Glimmer like glazed, yellow marbles. "I'm
Exhausted, for we've been at war with Orion," he pauses,
"But I don't know, in this Life,
Which wars are worth waging"

Spacetime warps and brings me back to an
Insoluble evening at Monkey Bar
Not far from where we worked together at McKinsey and
Where buildings aged slowly like trees
You said 'the tectonic plates shift at night' as pink
Clouds of mass delusion
Mantled the horizon line, eliding meaning
A storm raged within my spleen. We rushed to

RENEE DE LA ROCHE-ZHU

Interpose something

Enduring between us and the insurgence of

The corporate quotidian. You see, I felt we struggled with the same thing –

The danger of being 'old folks'

At twenty-three

You crystallize into a dot as I set my watch for the

Duration it takes to migrate from excitement

To apathy. I look up at the stars again, only

This time, I see the portrait of our twenties –

How your eyes flicker

And your mouth moves to urge me to

Quit my job before Christmas Eve

Don't I know it – as if Anne Sexton could play

By the rules

Now I will grow my own fruit. My face is calm

As a mannered sea

I get off the Merry Go Around of this Earth, riding away

From the extinction scene

Sedona, November 2023

THAT SUNDAY, THAT SUMMER

Even in spring, the LA sun loads its own guns – along
Colorado Boulevard dogs and humans breathe
In atoms of a mountainous surety
A sea of blooming petals unnerves me
I go hide in Restoration Hardware for a moment of
Respite, except I have a software problem – decorative
Plants – they chant, too – like reclaimed
Wood, about 'new beginnings.' Surrounded by white women
Picking out new couches
At 3pm – the apparent hour for fresh
Striped linens
Fazed by the hopes of being transported
Somewhere different

The alien fleet moves into our orbit today – the man
Said grimly on CNN. I turn it down as my phone flashes
With news of the earthquake in Hong Kong
The home of homes – if the heart of hearts
Could ever find it again
A sliver of regret rises to the tip of my tormented
Psyche – I feel it this time –
The tides of hurt that I wasn't there, until the fridge

Sirens for being kept open far too long
And sweet & sour pistachios rain down from the ceiling –
There aren't going to be enough snacks for doomsday! I slam
It shut as the news anchor warns us
Of imminent contact. But you don't see it. You say to me,
Sweet baby, the steak is ready

They don't know I know this – but my father is aboard that spaceship
Sleeping in silence, head tilted
Sideways this moment
Through my special glasses I watch him breathe and think:
When is he going to die?
Will the second time hit me
Like lightning? The Nietzschean mess around him
The smallness of him
Against the vastness of the spaceship bed
For I was not a 'sweet baby' when I played my first
Symphony – I bribed the maids to get out of practicing
Time coagulates in my throat
Bitter
Like honey

Until the alarm on my phone alerts
Me of spring cleaning – I settle into it, slowly
Dust has collected everywhere. Oftentimes the question
At the core is – 'where do we begin'
Indeed. Where did we begin? Newspaper stacks
Set aside, ready to be burned, like our books, too
My hair on the floor meanders like the spiral of
My DNA to the Cultural Revolution,

OUR LIFE BEFORE MARS

And then 213BC – Qin Dynasty
Then back to the Urth Caffe, except the voice in my head
Is that of Nat King Cole's, *That Sunday,*
That Summer. Then and now, in this dark forest with
Two moons
You can be someone new, too

Los Angeles, March 2024

QUAIL EGGS

I can't behave – my weather still overwhelms
The hour of dawn, then dusk – carving epic poems
Onto my inner wrist
Neither dismal, nor
Romantic
I lay my body down under a violet sky

And think of death – ordinary like
Making breakfast. Six cracked quail
Eggs
I catch a glimpse of you
One Friday night
Tick, tick, tick – your body dries up

In a grass coffin as you turn around and hide
From what we've come to know
As children
That the sun will desert us, and it will hurt more
Not less, to believe in the Big Idea
I watch you coalesce

Into a neutron star. I no longer expect
You to sing or journey Home
But the waves are landing

OUR LIFE BEFORE MARS

Differently this year

In my garden, white hydrangeas

Billow

Santa Monica, April 2024

PRESENTLY (SOON)

The letters dance in the wind – this time,
Without their formal synchrony
Literature feels lightyears away – nearby the shrubs
On Green St. draft spiderwebs of an unknown
Language – without verbs – and a Life, now,
Of quiet phenomenology

On the phone I rave to my mother about the new
Fava bean snacks I ordered
Like them, my shell's gone now. Perhaps,
Here is what I have lost – the veracity
Of the minute hand laboring on
A weathered, yellow-tinged face

But what I love, I have gained in spades
I poured my needs into the wild – until
words turn into the greenest
Moss of this wetland where the child is
Safe. Where creativity flickers on
Without an audience

Pasadena, June 2024

TRIP TO JAPAN

In Kyoto this time, I learned I had
Always known Buddha
Not as a friend, but as an acquaintance
The Arashiyama forest whistles
Nostalgically at me – emptying its guts in the evening
As my invitation gets lost
In a film actor's garden
Towards the peak
Tell me, are you also wondering
If we will ever go Home again

But the scenery seen once, and then for ever
Is the one already within
On the other side of the city
Lights flicker at the restaurants along the Kibune river
Impatient as the moon rises above the shrine
To illuminate the Face of one, and another lover
Of Summertime
Of impermanence
Here life takes on a different
Punctuation

On the train to Hakone I await
Volcanic activity of a disparate kind

The Shinkansen slows down its pace on my
Birthday. Could it be real this time?
The next best Nankai Earthquake
I want to be bound by it – the rituality of Onsen ryokans
Knowing that Death is omnipresent
And Life comes up for air as we submit to the
Ebbing grass fields of Sengokuhara

Somewhere in Tokyo I find my blue shadow
This time – next to yours
They dance like little children on the way to school
It is twenty-something years ago – and we are
Five, or six – this time in Shirokane
I scream at the top of my lungs as my favorite bakery
Runs out of chocolate hazelnut croissants
You calm me down with a familiar litany of cheek kisses
'Don't worry, we'll have some when we get home'
Perhaps we will have had always been home

Tokyo, August 2024

THE GAZELLE

Life is to be lived in chapters, you border on the cliché on
The phone calling from Switzerland – telling me some stories are
Left in pieces only for others to endure. The research is going well,
You say. I admire this patience of yours, for mine, it wears thin
On afternoons where the sight of the Pacific Ocean looms
Far as only a suggestion
In the distance anonymous jazz hums in the
Backdrop – beckoning to me
About the price of growing older and 'firmer', like how God
Summons in the animals, in pairs

Inner peace is never commoditized despite seeking to
Architect a life in this tranquil town. I took a sip from the 200th
Matcha latte I've ordered under the blazing sun – and tell
You it was almost five summers ago when we first met. We
Who were both born in the August sun and impatient about
Growing up into something with wings. We who both rejoice in
Duke Ellington and novellas on Sunday afternoons. Except as we
Got older – moments grew gelatinous and congealed into days, which
Flowered into congested months. The veracity of happiness
Outside the window started to feel borrowed, sublet

We reminisce about that July at Cambridge as I examine the
LA skyline outside the window. A chance encounter

That grew into a genuine friendship. An understanding. I stir
My drink and recall a collection of pub nights and punting, walks
In town. Was it Existentialism we talked at length about, or
Modernism? Were we afraid of our beating hearts? Perhaps
Both, for the waves were rising then, surely. But I keep
This thought from you like I guard my trade secrets – how I
Talked our way onto the lawn of King's College past opening
Hours. I remember not if the moon was out that night
But your saying something akin to, 'we'll go far'

The decision to leave New York is easy, but living with it is harder – I
Lecture you on the terms of adulthood – how they blister
Us like the sun, peeling our skin. *What are you reading lately*, you
Ask with a casual affection. "*One Man's Bible*," I answer
With alacrity – about how I charged through a story
On isolation and exile while I took shelter on Green Street –
Waiting for 6PM to arrive on the daily. For the UV index to drop
Below 4. You tell me you sent me a Cavafy poem, *The Old Man*,
And to remember that the right city will remain, like how the
Right person will stay. I stopped counting the days, as I
Once did in Tokyo, on the other side of the Pacific

Soon outside this tunnel of memories, and of endeavoring,
With the leaves changing and the sun less harsh – I will say
To the birds that I'm tired of being brave. *Do you remember
The train ride to Richmond – how we failed to locate Woolf's
House?* You ask with the singular aim to commemorate the
Hours. Suddenly I realize we are both members of the Institution
Of Dreaming, and that long ago what we've forged is a kinship

OUR LIFE BEFORE MARS

Of the mind that billows regardless of our weather. For this thing
Between us isn't a fragile thing to behold – it's a gazelle
Ready to gallop – through our thirties. Through time
The seasons that count

Los Angeles, October 2024

LOS ANGELES, THE CITY IN WHICH I LOVED YOU

LA, tell me something today
As I cried yesterday in bed with the thought
That I'm leaving you. This time –
Not forever, if I can help it
Chasing shadows on Green Street, passing by this
Convention, or another, as
Normality
Settles down over me. As the city wakes up for love
More than for work and money

LA, do you know I put this off for a while?
Articulating my sorrow – for I'm out of words
I've been stuffing myself with Ube coconut
Croissants from the bakery on Union Street
These past few weeks
High on refined carbohydrates, my sentence structures
Stagnated
Much like practical life, in a way,
Whilst I've been with you

But LA, sometimes it was difficult to tell the aches
In my career from the bruises on my skin

OUR LIFE BEFORE MARS

You impinged on me, didn't you?
With your glazing
Sun. I lived for a while in hatred of you. I hid, I hid
I sat in Ubers from Pasadena to Beverly
Hills
Cursing you – 45 mins never felt longer – I detested
The obscenity of your clogged arteries

LA, I was a provincial New Yorker with a cold little
Heart when we first met. Your vastness, perhaps
More impressive than Tokyo, was a map for another
Mechanism of life –
Mexican sushi in Silver Lake, walking down Sunset
Blvd. I'm not saying I'm not
Cynical
Anymore, but I'm in love now – the best matcha latte
And taiyakis I waited half an hour for in Japan town

LA, my Burmese hairdresser said she lives in Rosemead, you
See – I've still yet to visit, nor will she know that I'm
Leaving you. But in a way I think she knows
I booked my last appointment with her Japanese
Boss. Still, I drank the hot green tea she made for me
A few weeks ago, I went to a magnificent
Chinese
Buddhist Temple in Hacienda Heights – I said a prayer
For those I love, and somehow thought of her, too

But LA, why are you making this so hard?
For I've been the Other my whole life. Now you've

Shown me the bluebird of happiness – in every face I see
I recognize home
Surely in Tokyo I came close, yet it was you
Who crystallized the opposite of
Atomization
Now you are in the wind – flying my kite on Malibu beach – so how
Am I to unlearn this noble feeling?

LA, you have a homeless problem, but I've never felt
More at home than with you. Daughter of a ruthless capitalist
Owner of one-way tickets and multiple
Lenovo laptops. You've somehow engendered in someone like me
Notions of permanence
And I hate the sun. Love the rain. A woman who can't
Drive
So how did you do that – how did you
Unhide the shadows under my arm at the Getty?

LA, I know I still got places to go – over the
City National Bank branch I see little Asian and Hispanic babies
In strollers rolling towards Colorado Blvd
Perhaps their parents are taking them to Griffith
Observatory for a peek into their future. Yet in this moment,
In Pasadena, next to the
Planetary
Society, I wish so hard to pause space-time
To be here with you – even if we can only exist in silence

LA, your otherness completes me
Famished for meaning – laughed at by some for seeking

OUR LIFE BEFORE MARS

To find it with you. Yet the moment I set off for the Lunar Launch
Base, I'm punished by the flu for
Absence from you, useless for weeks
LA, I loved you in the city in which I loved you
Now I live in a new city on the moon in which I
Look
For you – where my body
Needs you – until I journey back to you again

Los Angeles, November 2024

III. NEW YORK / AFTER THE PANDEMIC

OF WITCH-HAZEL, THICKENING

Say, could we have commanded the Hours
Better? Probably, but it hasn't mattered
For a while. In me, then, the migration of the stars unique – the sun
Orbits Mars
You were, perhaps, capable of being my equator
In my dream we danced on oil-stained
Sandpaper – while elm trees conversed
With each other at night about our silent failures

You were darker than I remember
When I walked towards you, half past eight,
Standing on some busy
City street corner
And I thought about the last time you knelt under
My architecture of fluidity. How I listened
To the children playing outside – and the noise
In me grew louder, and louder, and louder

But the sun still set at our rush hour. Lying in
Your room, you revealed to me your secret – your
Every saved receipt and museum ticket, when I was your

RENEE DE LA ROCHE-ZHU

Favorite philosopher. Your Nietzsche. Your
Schopenhauer. Before you wasted too much ethos on
HBO Max – '*The Staircase*' – or grossly overestimated your
Own importance climbing some finance ladder, muddling fact with
Fiction – mistaking mediocrity for heroism

Your letter came in the mail – but I didn't bother to open it
For your words were empty bombshells at
Best, weren't they? I closed my eyes towards
The figures of beauty, and thought I was
Dreaming. Until the music from the living room
Sounded like a stream. But it isn't
A dream. Just the sound of *you* living on
Life's peripheries. Of *my* witch-hazel, thickening

New York, March 2025

THREE LIVES

As LA burns across the continent, and
In the heartland of my sensibilities – I took off
This time from Boston, frigid yet steady, for New York –
The city that once gave me my second life
And the living of it, in equal measure
For a while now, inadequate. Fading, like a thin
Sheet of smoke with the veracity of
Darkness, from view

How have I managed my way to another Manhattan
Blizzard, as I did every other – beholden to
The cold. I charge. I charge. I take off my face paint to sit by
The familiar windows of my favourite Village
Café. A stranger walks up to me asking if I were 'Claire'
New baristas with pink hair clamor over the counter
Offering me neighborhood discounts – even though I'm
No longer a regular

My friends give me the most wonderful present – being
Available last minute – dinner at L'artusi, lunch at Le Coucou,
Neon nights in Brooklyn. In these moments something in me says this
City can still run in my veins – until my aesthetician at the
La Prairie spa went on a diatribe about 'men in New
York.' I wish I could send a manifesto to all women to pledge

RENEE DE LA ROCHE-ZHU

Allegiance to the wrinkles on their clavicles – the gaps
Between their teeth – for they are, our only, living country

Thirteen years in Manhattan – not long enough
To be a full lifespan. Except in dog years we'd have gone
From strangers to lovers – married now in some quaint
Townhouse – if you'd been courageous enough to
Admit what you really wanted was
More of what I am
You sit at the Met now where *La Bohème* is not
An opera – but a Lifetime

And that it is poetic justice that you'll never know that I, too, battled
With the fear of happiness, the age we learned to be bystanders
To the advent of the morning – how it wears the war on its
Shirt sleeves. How it eats glass for breakfast. How I also
Took out one, and then many insurance policies against my fragilities
Even before I stepped out your door, knowing I had outgrown
The architecture of you. You who were
Unable to call the quotidian by its name

The third time – a bookstore, perhaps, or an oyster
Bar. I looked for silent planets that burned through
The night – not comets, inconsistent and ugly. Like how you
Were full of it. Like how I was unmoored by the non-identity
Of youth, with strengths you could never match. Just as I now
Know – I wouldn't have returned even if we had
Three lives. And I wouldn't have missed you
When we are dead

OUR LIFE BEFORE MARS

New York, January 2025

FRENCH RESTAURANT

Back in New York, I think I fractured your light
Once upon a story
It refracted and echoed down the city streets
Arched like a cat –
Once waiting for Life, past and
Present
Life that tells us what we want. Yet now the future
Can't arrive fast enough
I draw in the photons as they hasten
I feel my twenties passing through me like a breeze
I feel it passing
Ceaselessly

Out of the kernel of darkness I sprang
From the hard-boiled edge of this world
Towards words of alternate eventualities
Hungered for the colossus of Hunter S. Thompson
To die at my hands
Arrogance – it pinches my nerves
I once told you,
At the height of our cynicism and our
Premature aging, they are
Lampshades made of black onyx
Sagging in zero gravity, not even

OUR LIFE BEFORE MARS

Thirty

Sometimes aboard a spaceship I notice
The violence of the blue sunset mantling the horizon –
In these moments I pause
To think of Earth
And of you
In flashes
We were not yet twenty-four
We were pre-World War III
We were rising like the October moon on your
Roof
Young enough then to know
Everything

In this blinding light I breathe and remember our history:
I see you, beckoning to me about a silly
Study or a dinner
French restaurant
The food is less than memorable
But we swirl in elation with those around us
You talk to me with a sweeter solace than the 'date' I leave for subsequently
From this vantage point I feel the moment and its enormity
Its timeless eyes
The cosmos glides past me
This time, we never stop being
Happy

RENEE DE LA ROCHE-ZHU

New York, January 2024

DAYS ON MARS

Along the sea, by the beach

Do you contemplate me –

And what's at the heart of things – is a question I don't need

Answers to; for I know you do

I have seen the likeness of you in ancient cave paintings

But when all the water evaporates, are these our last or first days on Mars?

Life here takes place at pace as I go to the farmers markets

On Saturdays. Still, the nights are cursed with two moons

When my darkness surges and the Martian storm takes you in –

Run the laundry machine, eat a piece of tea cake, and wait for it to end

On the journey here it looked like I've decorated the storyboard with the big questions: The future of humanity –

But I'm consumed by the palpable fragilities of our life, here and back home

Somewhere else in spacetime, my father is a family man – in the front seat

Of his car, he asks me 'what would you like to eat'

As we drive towards Mercury; he turns up the radio, and asks me

To listen to the sound of a supermassive blackhole – 'do you hear Him?'

And I say, 'oh'. He says, 'I know'

No one awaits us at home except a singularity

RENEE DE LA ROCHE-ZHU

The light fades into my bedroom, two sixteen

Dreams embody me – I travel in waves of subconsciousness, foaming

Towards yellow-collared orange tulips

But will there be safety on this sterile planet in each of the ways I exist and breathe

Will you learn to paint every fragment of me and my being

Of my heart expanding, as time does, over the surface of an insensate galaxy

New York, May 2023

IT WAS LATER THAN I THOUGHT

In my days at 123 Washington silence grows

Like vines, with fortitude and a solemn numbness in equal measure

Next to these crisp windows it swallows me completely

For the sun comes up every day, but is it only a habit, like love

My heart, however, sometimes I seem to feel it sink along the horizon lacerated with red

And orange wounds – is this where I'll meet

My mother this time, or myself, if I'm not careful

I walk up West Street aimlessly

With a cold stoicism and openness to possibilities

That I'm not unused to – but, I wonder:

How is this trail different from Piccadilly

Or Kioicho-dori, against which I ran with a red comet

Inside my womb towards the light rain at dusk –

With tremulous breaths – the perpetual earthquake of my Imperial Palace

Yet today I must be the furthest from Tokyo I've ever been

Closest to Antarctica, and its frigid rule of law

It feels like just yesterday I sat for my portrait, violets

In my hair, hope steaming in my veins, naked yet white hot in my diaphanous dress of ivory

RENEE DE LA ROCHE-ZHU

No – this version of life – it isn't enough

When travel ceases – I work the graveyard shift for not one but two

Lives. The rush of silence fills the sweet, deep throats of this 56th floor aquarium which I now call home

So, the fish swim, the Ukrainian war rages on, and I make chia pudding

Useless, glittering like the dark face of the moon. I watch the Fed

Hike rates as I turn up the *Grateful Dead*, but I cannot turn

Off the darkness. The antidote to reality is not escape, or dreams, but the passage of grief, surging and

Falling – yet I still wait for humans to go stay at the Mars hotel

And if this were the end of our Climate, I want only a balcony of white roses, Sylvia Plath poems to spend

Forever to read, and the chance to ask for a new planet to be from

Criminalized like red placenta, my thorny personality still chafes against the palette of the many

But I've ridden a riptide far and long enough

To look up and contemplate God – how I'm not like him when he eats me like Jesus

Is it the ocean you hear in me? Its mercuric endlessness

Now I see the places and people that build me up, twenty-eight-feet tall, just to tear me down

Lay my head down in a hotel or an alien spaceship. I do not fear it. I've been

To heaven – where the stars plummet to their just address – my most earnest arteries

New York, January 2023

GIRL FROM THE PALE BLUE DOT

I'm back at Café Kitsuné again, this time, comfortable
With the colossus of my past –
I ride the 1 train passing by Canal Street,
Then Houston – while the phone screens around me, like in a cinema,
Are lit up with the minute vicissitudes
Of our silent voyage

'An espresso for Gavin', screamed the pink-haired barista
Now words grow gelatinous – to create a new Constitution
They are no longer enough
On Charles Street a new family eat and speak about the war at my old dining table
I pick up my last few letters and packages, and I'm like –
When will it be my turn to forward them to Mars?

You ring me from California
I put on my new furniture and the clouds –
There's a girl who still likes the song that goes 'Once I wanted to be the greatest'
You say of course you know – we talk about the constitution of nostalgia, new food
recipes, getting direct sunlight, and my
Annus horribilis. You ask, is this frigid sky capsule home that I built for

RENEE DE LA ROCHE-ZHU

a new start

Increasingly my heart

The news flash on my phone casually – did you know

That pulling out of the climate alliance is Vanguard?

That he is writing the next best English novel, or not –

It doesn't even matter, you see – all fiction is good fiction when it makes your voice break

In this life we are still in need of thunder and rain on some foreign boulevard

A black cat in the street corner tells me she's not afraid of losing

Her hair when she looks at the portrait I drew of her one day at age 33 and 45

She insists I'm as she is, like Voyager – in need of only a bouquet of flowers, a journal, and a view of the stars

I say, throw in a mini-fridge, please – let me have it as my night- and daylight, and a portal

To the future and the past

With my foot off the gas now, little girl, Goodbye until Andromeda

New York, December 2022

PRINCE GALLERY HOTEL, À LA ANNE SEXTON

In my dream, sinking into the blue marrow
of the skeleton of my colossus
My real, unimpeded dream
I'm running up and down Kioicho-dori
In sweat I search for a street sign
that hangs above the river at the Prince Hotel
"Jazz here tonight, Black & white moonshine"

I walk in a yellow dress on Bleecker Street
And a black pocketbook filled with makeup,
enough excuses, my work phone, and wallet
And on the edge of twenty-five, or is it forty-five
I pace, I pace
I hold up matches at street signs
For I've crossed a line

I have lost my orange typewriter
And a father who has wiped off his eyes
In order to take me at my surface curvature
Walking, and looking, and walking again – this is not a dream
Just my life

Where I'm running out of alibis
And the hotel is unfindable for a lifetime

I open my black pocketbook
As women do
And sharks swim between the dollars and lipstick,
and between the dead skull of the miserly & shallow man I once lay my head next to
And the good men for whom I put the killer in me to sleep in front of a glass mirror
In my life I live
In the waves I stay asleep, but breathe

Note: Written in honor of Anne Sexton's "45 Mercy Street"

New York, October 2022

A WOMAN IS A WOMAN

July it is again – clouds gather on my mind

And in the lathering thickness of my matcha latte

In West Village summer tourists frolic amongst vapid insta-thots

And third-rate marketing professionals

As Bleecker Street flows downtown, reeking like an incandescent river of dross

It's hard not to ask – but what has the Village

Done to itself? And what have I

Done to myself? I've lost my special edition dark sunglasses

After the cleaning lady came last week – but did I also the two years

Whilst I've had them since I came back from Tokyo?

On the sixtieth-something floor of WTC a few aggressive men ask me

Questions they do not want real answers to

Anger and condescension line my black pockets

They seek to arbitrate the rights of my voice, and my body eventually –

My procession to the grave

In my closet my dresses stay up all night conversing with my trousers

Not knowing I can hear everything – the soundtrack of my

Extinction if I stay put. The grey veins of the Moon – running within which not blood

But detergent

I wait for a complete statement of my actions

RENEE DE LA ROCHE-ZHU

This is what living hell feels like – this waiting after you'd been passed over

It feels and tastes like chalk powder, irritating your throat

The uncertainty of death hangs upon my bedframe and looks at me with a casual eye

The banality and ugliness of vacuous men suffocate me

On this dead leaf of a street I'm a woman shark out of water

New York, July 2022

J.W.M. TURNER

Spring, the one in me with wilted cherry blossoms, comes as you bring me a book

Named *Pulse* – it is my funny failure, I say

Holding up this mirror, in which you

Look back at me like a far sea with history, thick as blue gravy

You are no more a child than the sky is bored on this April afternoon – you stand

With a knot in your stomach as you loosen your shoes

In the morning in West London, my father was just a man

I now eat men like him

For breakfast – a restless train runs

Over his body, and he is out of view like smoke, while on a far shore horses

With a terrible hardness lay down to die

I consort with angels – drumming up and down his bones

I was a woman once upon a white cliff or two

I'm tired of reading my mother's travel journals – I've walked through cities, and then miles of

News that lately make me blue

Without a map – or as the French say – a "plan"

I am almost

Someone going homewards to you

RENEE DE LA ROCHE-ZHU

Boston, March 2022

IT'S LONELY TO BE ON EARTH NOW

It's lonely to be on Earth now – do you know that, Major?
Building this ship of fools to
Escape to Mars. The fluorescent light in meeting
Rooms draws on my inflammation, in this lone star state,
Or another, underneath which I spin
In flashbacks when you were humming *Suzanne*
The day I left you, father. Until the captain announced we were
Making our descent into this tapestry of arteries
Constituted of lights and love that
Go missing

In my dream I walk towards the green sea
That crystallized these learned and
Noble feelings
I stand on every balcony of every hotel room, the clouds
Glistening atop a burning sunset – but why do I now
Feel nothing? All I can think of with concreteness
Is my fridge light – how it waits for me –
Regards me with certainty when I was confounded by
Artificial boundaries – that of ourselves and our nation states. Like you
Once were, traversing through the world in different languages

Near the Seven Sister Cliffs you discuss the lightness
Of eternity
I solemnly declare eternity bores me, at age 6
It's a Bank Holiday – little poppies dance on
My skirt and my lips
We eat and swirl at a picnic – you say today
I can have loads of chocolate sweeties
The 'Froggie frog' kind
While I'm making a big red balloon disappear
Into my little fist

Except now everywhere I go, your face wrinkles and
Bulges before me like scenery
The life support machine beeps – I think it sounds like
Singing. But I'm not a smile, daddy
I can't erase the darkness that envelops me
Develops me
I travel in space like electromagnetic waves – I've been
Burning on both ends, a woman without a home –
What you wanted me to be
I rise, I fall – I have nothing, yet everything I wanted

Houston, January 2022

IV. NEW YORK / DURING THE PANDEMIC

MY FUTURE

One day Manhattan will submerge within me
My heart redolent of the vivacious past it carries
The beauty who is at once the beast
The little girl in the mirror at one with her womanly being
All within my suitcase and me, just the two of us
Racing up Queens
To fly to India, or somewhere else hot where the stars never fall asleep

In this new regime I will breathe differently
I will make, and comfortably take, until there are trees
Everywhere in my garden – and I will teach, though words are not enough –
They can form cities, until my eyes can see
More clearly than ever the beauty of deserts, and not of oases
Not because of what had been, but what is always to come
My happiness is like water – omnipresent, flowing like a consistent stream

The hours pass – and at the end of the realm of themes
I find a room of my own – because life is of the particulars:
My Sylvia Plath and Virginia Woolf stacks, sundresses, and scattered paper with my writing
I forage and make bouquets of orange tulips
They blossom next to glass doors while my terrible eggplant burns in the oven

OUR LIFE BEFORE MARS

But it doesn't matter – I'm not even hungry
I prefer to dance to scratched records that skip

Under the stars the winds fray my nerves slightly
But I regain my composure as I listen to the leaves
I will keep looking for the remains
Of the earthly storms within me
And unlike Andromeda I won't wait for Perseus by the cliffs
I will listen to the voice in my head
Which all along had been my own under the sea

New York, July 2021

YOUTH

Summer streets come flooded with young, blonde girls in white tennis shoes

Reminds me of my mother when she was younger, crisper, but harboring more truth

My hair, however – it is a lot darker –

And my heart, too, with a palpitation that rings deeper

Than the canonical verses that decorate the contours of youth on another day in June

She said he threatened to leave when she screamed in Calcutta under the moon

A silence envelops me, develops me – all that was misconstrued in the monsoon

No, I can't help now but wonder –

Did she simply get sick of her jewels or run out of sandpaper

On which to fictionize him, "Mr. Win to Lose"

I wait anxiously for the crimson waves to bring me the news

At night they rush into my brain – my being and spirit washed away like the fake sand dunes

I built that year when I was smaller, where the sun looked brighter, and I didn't yet know my brother

I'm on that beach again but does it matter – in your novel you made me better

I still long for the West African coast but hunt for a moment of rest before boarding another Ship of Fools

In my most poetic dream, we check into the only hotel on Mars and dance in my room

Filled with white hydrangeas – we go fly fishing in Utopia Planitia, you say I have the wrong tools

For you are my witness, tell me I need not forgiveness and safeguard what remains of my tenderness

I could leave everything on Earth behind, even their verdict and my solitude

I still don't know how long a moment is, but I will travel to where only the sunset is blue

New York, June 2021

SO LONG, MS. FIRST AID

I've been listening to the same wretched
Song for ten wretched days
You asked me for a clean slate – and if spring
Had taken shape in post-pandemic
New York the way I had said I wanted – on which
Lies my own face
With no trace of the past – the sordid, say, the British
Museum – effaced, set ablaze

When I heard about you, brother, I was a womanchild
Who swindled in the art of being away. In my ear
Resounded the waves, and the frailty
Of being brave on a constantly emptying stage
On the phone my mother explained, "of needing to go, but
Choosing to stay"
I think I believed her as I got taller – so I placed my hand on
Your desolate moors as the Tokyo earth quaked

I was on the run, still, I paused in the waiting
Room when your blood stained my pillowcase
And like you, I break down then fashion the
Seasons into a new statue, despite the Siege of Calais
We watched *Cathy Come Home*, but you have to go now,
I know, I know. You said not all was in vain. Yet you still fogged up

OUR LIFE BEFORE MARS

The mirror in Union Square Café, "don't say goodnight
To the bad guy" – were you talking about daddy or Scarface?

Is it too soon, or too late to replace the bullets
In my gun case – and paint a portrait of mid-May –
The imminence of the naked certainty yet
Abruptness of heatwaves
Lay me down softly, as you never had a chance to do
In our separate childhoods. Sing me a
Heartfelt lullaby – soon I'll draw up the license to
Shine from words in a one-woman parade

We've missed the forest for the trees
From a young age
Here, and everywhere, when I look up at the moon
I see his face
Weathered, now lined in pain
But perhaps you'll be right beside me, in a way,
Transmitting from the weathervane as I learn to escape
The Escape of our Age

New York, May 2021

BETELGEUSE, SEE YOU AT SUNSET

Could someone show me how
A play, or two, that need not flop
Against exotic landscapes chorus singers chanted "forget me now"
To stay, when you have left – is to be within, and do without

So, say, what are the odds
That I close my eyes and see only a field of white hollyhock
April raindrops, unlike earthquakes, hit me like polka dots
Disappearing onto the pavement before the aftershock

Leaping into a meteoric downpour from atop
Can I let myself stay tender as Georgia O'Keeffe or should I stop
Around my neck tightens Orion's belt – the tune that rushed into my chest mellows out
Is this a dream, or is it not?

New York, April 2021

VAGUE D'AZUR

(Azure Waves)

Perhaps one day I will stop listening to Phoebe Bridgers
Within me time goes faster – then slower
When I chase it – the truth comes closer, then further
The night falls, I try to make sense of it all –
The Martian light grows only darker
where Ulysses sails the metaphorical water –
"Were you just another wild guess for the Tokyo reporter?"
Until the sun sets in Gibraltar, be a page-turning thriller
fading into the ether
I'm still the blower's daughter

New York, April 2021

風の歌を聴け

(Hear the Wind Sing)

Thomas called from Cannes one afternoon and said he's living on his boat, and something

half-ridiculous like "onwards to Africa, my banjo & your typewriter, no more blues"

For the second time that week in a drugstore lane I caught myself laughing

and pictured Paul Weller on a Citibike humming *My Ever-Changing Moods*

See, you think I'm Jo March, not "Sylvia Plath with her *Bell Jar*", living without gravity

But I – I turned the corner and almost forgot our bet about the next best Bombay monsoon

Three or four songs repeating in a loop on the interstate

I wanted to say I know you, and it's not too late, or too early to write a brand-new tune

But when the moment came I hesitated,

because I'm a liar, and I'm unsure how to interrogate the absurdist facets of our youth

and how I think I could go anywhere with him, even home, though perhaps I didn't want to – and in the dark you kept asking

has it been an eternity, at the movies, or a moment since we were twenty-two

You say it's ok if I change my mind again and move across the world, and collide

with satellites that are bound to find and miss a winter harvest moon

I saw you through the window that day – and I felt something – like passing flights

that glide through the skies, because I want to be consumed by a relentless storm in June

and wake in every extra-ordinary morning to a Schopenhauerian light – that of the depth of night

My father once told me nothing solid ever melts into air or fades from view

At the departure gate he kept saying he'd come with, and that's not what I wanted to hear

Though in a way it's what I always want to hear, but I don't want the stillness on the roof, or to be your Waterloo

25 felt like hallucinating, elated, out of air

Travelling in technicolor mists, to find an avalanche, or a breakthrough

And when I'm with her again in the chalet, dancing to French tunes I can't bear

We run out of vermouth, and she says it's time I fell from the news into the truth

Because one night when the traffic light turned red you asked me to stop swimming

against the tide and stay, if I could, in Xanadu

But I was an acrobat, a diplomat who followed my head, left you a note saying nothing

except that I shall see you again when all is golden in hue

And I haven't left your mind since

An excuse – tabooed – a ruse – I'll be breaking all your countrymen's rules

RENEE DE LA ROCHE-ZHU

Geneva. December 2020

GEORGIA O'KEEFFE, MS. ALLERGIC TO CHEESE

Next to sleeping willows, I realize I may not be a storyteller

Plots and characters are stagnating, like joint pain

I know not how to weave or untangle webs of interconnected words, last July or another

And punctuations, as my orange typewriter

Runs out of black ink

But in the afternoons, I forget about the hardship of barely

Walking up Bleecker and passing by Sullivan Street, and of not knowing you

So, I swallow whole a ham with French Dijon baguette sandwich

You're getting older, aren't you, in the street corner of my mind

And when the sandwich gets spicier in taste – should I keep it a secret or tell you?

The October wind passes through me, or is it the other way around?

When I think about the little Daikanyama hills, your steadfast shadow

Under a building of four closed restaurants – later I knew it was a National holiday

This is far from the only story up my sleeve, but I want to write about it

And to tell you, I had gone back there to buy a white suitcase to carry my dresses and poems

But I'm out of pretty words, or

Connectors that make prose into song

I have only red bricks, grey walls of the architecture of my honesty

Facts – the dusk light of the night, of everywhere, for they are really the same

The weightlessness of me and of Fall

If I were only honest, I had never within

Me more than a meter of greenery

I stood up trees, and then forests, for you – and decorated the brick walls with pictures – as normal people do

Now I live with the remnants of a revolution

I read the Marxist Terms of Service, my head next to my species being when I cannot sleep

I bury you in the quotidian flickering of lights – traffic noises near the water – and digital copies of the FT

In the oven my dying green plant is marinating with my last boy's shaving cream

I once said – less is not more, yet less is enough

Well, that's what happens when you give a twenty-something the weight of thirty-something's

Most of the days I'm a stream-of-consciousness Georgia O'Keeffe – I'll build a wall and cut it down daily with the ones who quietly comprehend my inner scream

The girl next to me in the waiting room said she'll call her mother when the sun sets

I'll google what that means –

As a schoolgirl I never had packed lunches, and now as a woman I live without a piano, and my apartment is a Nietzschean mess

There are thoughts you can't clean but that's alright – I no longer live with the imminence of a mining disaster

A hotel room is where I belong – says Google Translate this fine

morning

New York, October 2020

SWEET AS SUMMER, THEN SWEETER

You wrote me a poem called summer

Running across the red poppy field I get wet and go skinny dipping in the river

Did you know at midnight it runs backwards?

Unlike time, kissing gladiators in St Germain and Westminster – now a new era on Bleecker

I always put on Michel Legrand when the stars grow dimmer

Sinking into a Godardian anarchy on apricot-stained writing paper

The waves surge in my mind & the boat catches on fire as we reached Martha's Vineyard

I dance to *That I Miss You* until we collide with a Sputnik sweetheart – a wonder, I wonder

They say I'm good at being brave – still, it rains – sometimes I get so tired of it I leave things scattered

So knock on my door with the Truth, disarm me like an easy-rider

Come as a devout Humbert Humbert, or a tenacious sailor – not a Knight in Shining whatever

Make me into something as sweet as summer, then sweeter

New York, August 2020

DREAM A DREAM, HERE'S A SCENE

In my dream you are never thirty
Running along the Seven Sisters beach
Whispering Sexton's poetry. You laugh and
Call me a "wild
Thing." The clouds of Roppongi gather with a sense of
Urgency – I am glad it masks my hesitancy,
And then melancholy. I say, when father called, "I fought
Against the current." Flying to New York
In a heartbeat

But change, how it grounds me and then
Confounds me – a city now without forests
Or deserts
The undercurrent of the past hums with a
Dream-like quality. Caught in a seismic shift, no longer
Who I used to be
For I thought yesterday was
Forever, but forever is thirteen hours away – a Tokyo
Film scene, sans sous-titre

In a floral robe portefeuille I bathe in a 'new
Beginning.' Red townhouses and carefree al fresco

Dining – do they harbor what I desire, the rush and depth of palpable
Uncertainty? Out of the blue I catch a glimpse of
Imperial Palace in the rain, the lights of
Marunouchi, Ibaraki earthquakes in my sleep
Till the sun pours into my window and
Wakes me from an alternate reality – tell me,
Will I one day be missing Charles Street, so intensely?

New York, July 2020

V. LONDON

YOU'LL EAT A HAMBURGER, IN FACT

Wake up anywhere, I used to see him in
Textured dreams. I could say I remember his kiss, sweet
Like soft ice cream. But I don't, for he's the remains of
A vanilla day called summer. New York, then
Eastbourne by the sea. Who cares, really,
About texture? Or flavor? When we converse
In different languages over breakfast, arguing
Over the color of sunrise. Over the distance between
Us and ourselves. For it changes,
Surely, as winter arrives, abundant in its anonymity
I walk down Piccadilly towards you now
Opening up, like my unadorned black dress for
New Year's Eve
At the seams

I take off and touch down, stranded in
Fragmented reveries. Sixty four times this
Past year, forgetting old sceneries. Outside this
Hotel, the cars rush past this restaurant and that – shuffling
People to theatres and cinemas. An ambulance siren
Blares. Over the bay, a steamer makes for the
Frigid sea. Are they running towards a fire?

OUR LIFE BEFORE MARS

Or away from a story? You say that's a better
Question for me, shaking your head
Like a man who makes his sorrow count. But I know
You are far from home. Far from your own name
For under the pavement, there are sands,
Bones, and
Seeds –

So I will eat a cornetto al prosciutto and throw all my
Shirts, silk, into the sea. No restaurants or clubs,
Just white daffodils by the kitchen sink. You'll
Take off my armor, Upper Belgrave Street or
Kioicho-dori. We'll toast to the petty fragments of life, and my
Piano-playing, very ill. And you can hold me close,
Say you want time to slow, and never goodbye, even when we
Run out of words, or when your tears run down my Achilles heel
You'll eat a hamburger, in fact, which you hate. You'll keep
On eating it, like how you'll keep on loving
Me. And I'll tell you it's ok if I don't
Get free, this time – and talk to
Your mother. No more wine to spill – until
My heart sinks no longer as we stand still

London, January 2020

THE ARROW

Back of any black cab
Or on the train aisle near you en route
to Bath – if I've killed one man, I've killed two
Now I see myself distill into
colors on every horizon
When the sun inevitably rises

Everywhere, and you speak from within the dim lights
in all my fridges, but not from the stage on which
I stand and look for commas – red like placenta.
In your old poems – our years never stiffened like my ribs,
now bruised with winter frosts, for they taught me Hope
Lately I stare at ceilings for their ghosts in search of you, waking up to my own

Because growing old
is a relentless yet sacred activity
I'm drawn to those who are ugly
and unafraid to see beneath
my riverbed of strength, on which I seek to become
a violet becoming – at ease with what sleeps within me

I've lost my mother's watch, but now I foam to golden collared waves
I have only the flowers on my dress, clamoring at the distinctive atrocity of sunsets

I rested my head at the eye of the cauldron as History tightened its
Bow
But this time, I
Am the arrow

London, December 2022

TED HUGHES

On the far side of the moon, my river Thames
Flows into yours, but the tides are teal and run smooth
With philosophical truths –
That of small rocks, and of the sky reticent in the rain
Whose horizon bleeds, and speaks to me in allegory
You are a fisherman that comes home with his nets
Wide and wet, and says – the last
Star on your dress, responsible for Mars' first sunset

In this vivid dream I essay to be braver at night
We jump into a chapter
That tastes like salted grains in a desert
Somewhere far but boisterous. We build a house near a gravestone
Without willows to strangle us with impermanent 'truths'
Alas, perhaps I have not met my Ted Hughes
Or have I – twelve or more years ago – when the equator
Encircled my continent whole

I throw my sneakers, sundress, and a lemon tart
Into a washing machine, followed by an ossified ventricle of my heart
I wait for a thunderstorm to swallow the past in a flood
For lightning to hit me as your warning does
You dive into my marrow
With the ease of eating an apple

OUR LIFE BEFORE MARS

In your words I am at once my reflection in the sea
And a new character on Piccadilly unbeknownst to me

London, March 2022

ARMY OF ME

(i)

Autumn arrived overnight, I say offhandedly on Bleecker Street

We didn't grow up here – we know not the tree rings to escape this Halloween maze

We were only sixteen when we thought we could be anything, and now

We are no longer at the party

Where the moon song was playing as you unscrewed the stars in Knightsbridge

I hated touching my spleen with you standing close to me

I say, like the summer rain this changes everything

In oatmeal textured dreams, I pick up *Ulysses* and read

My test results through technicolor Tom Ford glasses – unworn but dirty

They said I'm running low on hemoglobin that produces empathy

But my labs read, allergic to hypocrisy; perhaps the weather in New York is not damp

Enough to carry the colossus of me

A cloud of seismic shifts

Momentous

The zoologist in me told you

About the emerald green alewife swimming

In my kitchen sink –

the drain stopped working, the fish

Are poisoned with pea protein powder and old manuscripts

You didn't want to call in the bomb squad at 2am

So I turned up *Julia Jacklin* as I got on a plane and did not speak

(ii)

I walk from Mayfair towards the Embankment with answers

A hardline – I drew it myself this time

A storm is coming; I don't mind

A far sea moves in my ear and then towards my left ventricle – I am aware of my heart

The opening and closing of it, like doors

And the white doves, they may no longer sing

That's alright; I am letting them go, surly

In East Sussex, the mist hugs a setting sun above white cliffs like a canopy

No need for a hero in this sky – except for my words in the orange notebook

That I carry to cafes across oceans, towards another

Version of life – as the living of the old one fades from view

Like the brass waves next to Japanese akari bringing the past and future into sharper relief as they recede

My heels click on London pavements – but I'm made of warmth and salt like the sea

Will I ever see land again?

(iii)

I have come to know that the Tokyo earthquake alarms will forever ring in me

I came by those sceneries by accident, which may ossify into sculptures

But not my musings

Just as I know those days by the Prince Gallery

Will eventually fracture like my bones, and will scarcely come back to me

I preserve them, in silhouette and substance, until I find them again

Amidst the waves

But this poem, which punctuates time at the heart of me, delineates the war of my twenties and its myriad casualties

It may not even be a poem – do you see?

Just a handsomely lit Piccadilly of vowels and consonants

Tower Bridges of existentialist ideas – which flow through your arteries

Together with my lacerated, postmodern sentence structures on Squares of unequivocal candor –

Constitute this elaborate and now bare

Body of me

London, November 2021

DANCING WITH FATHER JOHN MISTY #2

In 2019 we were young enough to know everything

My guns were blazing

across Europe, and Tokyo drifting

Chasing a singular ideology I still look for silent planets that are burning

through an eternity

The waves were rising, and you say, now we're in the business of living

The sun – it also rises in the East

But men still perish in India, and some near Westminster Abbey

In a different galaxy

I traversed planets, consumed happily in a Leviathan tyranny

where the neon lights shone all night, layers of reality unfolding

in a rose-colored symphony – where I was one, and many, but never every

But summer, all wavered and bent against my home – the totality of New York City

Except "home" rang in my ears like an unspoken scream, gone from its normalcy

The adults kept talking,

but you wouldn't stop bleeding

So we flew – far – where I asked the lion in Trafalgar Square, seen once and for ever, for a prescription – a sense of meaning

Sometimes we roll down the blinds and wait for Life to hit us like lightning

Burn through the noise, leave only the truth – the best of me – the contours of my insanity, the ugly

The architecture of love is one of fluidity, like our youth, everchanging, fleeting

I put away your fragile verses in a carry-on for a trip to Mercury

Where the war is over if you choose, nothing to fear or lose – our hearts on our sleeves

The music in you, never-ending

London, September 2020

ONE DAY

In high school you bring me withering bouquets on racing day

In love with his beat poetry, my white tennis shoes, living in a Belgravian horseplay

The sun coats the Surrey polo field with gold, a star and her Ricochet

My wild temper, a raging sea, burning through a postmodern European decay

Two suitcases in JFK, a heart in a getaway car racing down West Side Highway

Morningside Hegel debates – swerving was our ambition, yellow cabs, and the ballet

Sitting for my portrait, as time alters my face, when forever was yesterday

Yet yesterday was *Hiroshima, Mon Amour* – a lifetime away

So I sailed close to Victoria Harbor, or Tokyo Bay

Talking philosophy, with his, and his hands on my waist

Finding out how my lipstick tastes, short stories become ill-adapted plays

The hotel rooms went still as the stage, the future, without a trace

I'll fly back to Manhattan and color spring in black Gaultier

Drifting back to a prince who'd been waiting with my crown in Union Square Cafe

In a kingdom downtown, Jackson Pollock served with my morning soufflé

RENEE DE LA ROCHE-ZHU

Making love on an ordinary Wednesday, elated by the heaviness of Mrs. Dalloway

And I'll wake up to clearer blue skies, while I lead you astray

Soft ice cream on my lips, a summer day, still I'd leave you for Johannesburg or Bombay

You don't fall in love once, or twice, but a thousand times, until your heart is on display

An apocalyptic genesis with a dash of out-of-context sadness, my forté

Tokyo, March 2020

VI. TOKYO

THE GREATEST

We embrace in Akasaka
A pallid silence crowds us
Say, you will remember the Fitzgeraldian parties
We peopled at twelve, half past
When you speak, you speak so substantially,
About your venture inwards, and towards Altair, Deneb, and Vega
Vowels and consonants – will you miss us – as roses miss white hydrangeas –
Seized in an Archimedean coup d'état

Traversing through the world with a wilderness in my heart,
A festival of cinematic yet quotidian imprints, details that last
Out of the many women growing in me I seek to make one,
A dance I'm learning to choreograph
In which I also make love to your quintessence – yet this, too, shall pass?
So indivisibly, in the style of Simone de Beauvoir
Yes, some people are in love
Some yearn for the waves at night, driving towards which in a car

"I'm a big girl," I said, so I did not tear up as I leapt off Tokyo Tower, but smiled
At our meta-modernism, on your behalf
Yet what is the past
If not what is unsaid – "don't leave – I just need a wake-up call" – a song you'd better not grasp

The moon is rising, the stars are burning, as the skyline falls in a basement Shinjuku jazz bar,

My heart both near and far

Happiness is a butterfly in August on a Newport morning, the sunlight harsh

Against the waters of my nostalgia I set sail – towards the thundering storm in your heart of hearts

Tokyo > New York, July 2020

AFTER THE AFTER

The thought of him – it used to linger

Like the bruises on my knee, growing darker, but then fader

Running past the imperial palace, an antiquated love, as my sun sets in his rush hour

The Roppongi neon lights against a neon moon, November – details, now vague as intergalactic dark matter

I once could write about him in a poem without pause or erasure

I dove into the deep blue waters of the night – the stars shifted as I came up for air – looking into the mirror at a serial killer

Are you in love or in pain, asked no one, ever

I said, "but what's the worst that can happen to a girl who's already hurt"

In a dreamland, I set sail towards a new answer

Create a different world order, have gun will travel, lead me to a story that is not proper

In it I'm unopened by a simple song, a 7am croissant, a never-ending summer

Catch me on the flipside in Kokomo, the Beach Boys on airplane mode – the here and now is after the after

Tokyo, May 2020

VILLEFRANCHE-SUR-MER

Say, can you fragment a fragmented heart

Sweet as vermouth, blessed with rage, the chamber of sadness ajar

Despite its scars, pretending to be brave in a postmodern Tokyo seminar

Surfing the Biarritz surge of my mind, as the skyline falls, like a shooting star

My sundress on the terrace, Serge Gainsbourg on repeat punctuated by Jacqueline François

Your suntanned fingers through my hair against a clementine-colored Villefranche – and the reckless chords on your guitar

Cold was the night, named desire was a streetcar, now all afar

On the cusp of such hope – sailing into the eye of the storm, despite warnings on the radar

Except the storm was within me – sitting next to him in a Fitzgeraldian bar, when I was once, then, truly in love

Tokyo, March 2020

LE GRAND BROUILLARD

In my heart there flickered a light called Central Park

Meandering were strawberry fields punctuated by middle eastern men at ice cream carts

When the future was as indivisible as sunsets on Fifth Avenue – a world not yet divided in half

But then came the current – our white boats foundered, lost in the reservoir

I think of New York most on moonless Saturdays, but like my lovers, they come and pass

Violence in Union Square, burning cars – flaming headlines that tear us apart

Our bodies once young and naked in the summer grass, now outgrowing chains that sought to define us

When does this chapter end, and where does the next one start?

Perhaps one never disentangles the mystery of love, whispered the dark surfer from Okinawa

When we thought lost were the stars, really, lost was us

The radio turned up on a scenic drive, *reste avec moi*

Imminent is the antichrist – a transvaluation – we are on the cusp

Tokyo, June 2020

GROUND CONTROL TO MAJOR GOLIGHTLY

You came to me in a manic pixie dream
Wearing the fabric of your subtleties
Laced with my imperfections, rainy nights in Roppongi
Ceaselessly, a heart of hearts, the taste is sweet as *Jules et Jim*

You think I'm beautiful – yet I'm not a prayer on your lips
But it is with words, dark notes, I cut deep into your skin
A play by Euripides, one of impossibility and blasphemy
Despite the daylight between us, you'd dance under my architecture of fluidity

Falling in love with me is a Ponzi scheme
But one day, when you ascend Mt. Fuji, think of me dearly
Imagine us kissing, the look on my face delicate, as we fall off the cliff
Away from this heartbreak city – into a restless sea

Tokyo, April 2020

SCREAM

You stood tall in a dark suit, an attitude of "all or nothing"

A kiss, unhinged, that of the 18th century

The rush of uncertainties running in my bloodstream

I want something bizarro and bleak – 6am crows of Roppongi

A shattered glass – a whisper in your ear, "*je n'suis pas d'ici*"

Making love to an impermeable metamodernity, L'Impératrice on repeat

Tokyo, March 2020

TOKYO BELLE DE JOUR

Falling in love
Is like humming *Crimson and Clover*
Dreaming of a brunette Catherine Deneuve
Climbing Mount Fuji in February without gloves

Akasaka nights, I bathe in silver stardust
We sway to the silence, frosted by winter illuminations in Ginza
Waking up to *Norman fucking Rockwell*, no makeup
You say less is not more, yet less is enough

Guilty until proven innocent, awaiting the judge
Your heart atop an ume branch, next to a white dove
Frontpage stories we do not discuss, oh, my blood
Drinking English Breakfast Tea at the noisy Tokyo American Club, à bout de souffle

Tokyo, January 2020

TOKYO, MON AMOUR

The sun rises in the east this time – unapologetic,

Like me. I wake up to a Tokyo oasis, punctuated by storied buildings

The contour of Mt. Fuji dances on the horizon – it speaks to me

Only in allegories – I think we are as close as we've been

In whirlpools I swim and look at clouds that remind me of the life I once gave away

Time passes as I resist the birth of this new poem

And its multitude of meanings, as sceneries and streets

Crystallize within me – I'll be in trouble if I let the physicality of Tokyo Tower enter my body

I walk abreast friends in Roppongi or Shinjuku, but I am my own blue shadow

Under the moon, I silence the sirens – I keep up this charade

How again after years there is the survival of details

And the feelings that encase the next best Tokyo earthquake – it has yet to arrive

Like my best poem. I live to be an archeologist to excavate the portion of life that takes place commensurate to our courage

No, I am not better at 'living' than I was three years ago

But I want to light up my dashboard to travel to the landscape at the end of me – to make my own way in the world

In a different universe, where the cherry blossoms

Bloom in the depth of summer under a violet Akasaka night sky

OUR LIFE BEFORE MARS

I am perhaps someone, with a grocery list in my hand
For fresh fruits and flowers, 8PM on a Tuesday
Walking homewards to you

Tokyo, July 2023

VII. HONG KONG

SOUVENIR

My love, I said, take me to the lights
In your eyes, dictated by silent planets of the night
Diseased with sadness, but with a vision, we stood under the tall elm trees

With a prescription, you were Edwardian, and erudite

Time was moving, through you, against a pallid grey sky

Aged and faded, summer evenings and our fluorescent gunfights

The waves were rising, and now we are living

And commemorate you will, our most ordinary, Sunday morning stage fright

Hong Kong, July 2019

HUNTER S. THOMPSON

You wrote three lines of poetry, painted me blue

Pierced through my thoughts, and our sonorous tune

The silhouette of my existence, searching for the roses on my dress upon my bed

Driving in your car, The Beach Boys, wandering down the avenue

I said, be wild, but fear the war I'm waging inside of you

A novel from start to finish, we paced, and around us, violet fumes

But happiness, it comes in waves, like the way you tune the radio

Till the coastline grows obscure, one song to choose

London, August 2019

THE LIFE BEFORE US

Sunday afternoons – they no longer rush into my windows

Like waves – they are quieter these days, you say

And time, it can bend sideways – turns out I left morsels of me on different continents

Some I can only find again when I return to them

When it rained in New York yesterday

I picked up the phone and rang the travel agent

For a ticket to myself. She said, 'sold out for this week – for the one-way'

CNN is on, and I make chocolate baked oats as the knowledge

Of our mortality inundates me. I think of Chinese fish that can't swim

In the Pacific – they work as conductors on the transcontinental

Underwater subway, breathing in the dollars until the structural integrity

Of our trading framework disintegrates

For this is how being bi-cultural punishes us –

We are privy to the hypocrisy of our personal history and that of our nation states

Now I'm finally on this flight – you'll be there when I land, but if not, that's ok

The runway is cleared for takeoff, unlike my brain

I watch the seatbelt sign go on and off in the hanging gardens of

Babylon. The pilot asks on the radio as they serve us fisheye gel with caviar,

'Is life sad but beautiful, or beautiful but sad?' So I thought, does it matter anyway

If I were heading to Hong Kong, New York, or outer space?

Will there be photos of me and my mother in my room tonight and when I hit replay?

And that one day I will learn that there is time, and then its malleability

It is what tethers me to the ground – my mother and motherland, my flesh and blood

– Yet it also sends me to impossible summits. A train

Thunders across the mountain ridge, mating as they give birth, shrieking

The equator encircles us and readies itself to be our God

Time ticks and licks my inner wrist as the river carries us home in its rambunctiousness

I'm youthful and ancient, all at once, in the crepuscular womb of daybreak

Hong Kong, August 2023

The End

AFTERWORD

"I know this much: that there is objective time, but also subjective time, the kind you wear on the inside of your wrist, next to where the pulse lies. And this personal time, which is the true time, is measured in your relationship to memory."

-- Julian Barnes

ABOUT THE AUTHOR

Renee De La Roche-Zhu

Renee de la Roche-Zhu (author of French Restaurant, Liminal Press, March 2024) writes at the intersection of existential dread and perfectly folded linen napkins. Shaped by a global upbringing and a professional life spanning academia, business, and the arts, her work explores identity, memory, and the fragility of the human  condition, weaving the philosophical into the everyday.

She graduated cum laude from Columbia University with a B.A. in Philosophy and Economics-Mathematics – a combination that explains both her metaphysical curiosity and her affection for "shareholder value." She began her career in investment banking at Goldman Sachs and later became an Associate Partner at

McKinsey & Company in New York, having lived and worked across the U.S., Europe, and Asia.

When not writing or contemplating the end of civilization, she advocates for elephant conservation, overuses her Japan Rail Pass to reach onsen and ski towns, and works as a corporate strategist.

BOOKS BY THIS AUTHOR

French Restaurant

Our Life Before Mars

www.ingramcontent.com/pod-product-compliance
Lightning Source LLC
LaVergne TN
LVHW041338080426
835512LV00006B/519